Sissy Bear at the Fort

By Holly Arnold Kinney

aka "She Who Naps With Bears"

Illustrations by Christina Wald

10 9 8 7 6 5 4 3 2 1

Printed in China by Imago

ISBN: 978-0-692-73761-3

Library of Congress Registration Number: TXu 1-998-236

Dedication

I dedicate this book to the many Fort guests who continue to share their stories with me of Sissy Bear at The Fort; and to their kids and grandkids who come to The Fort, often bringing their toy Sissy Bears to tell me of their adventures with a friendly bear!

I also dedicate this book to my wonderful husband, Jeremy Kinney, who encouraged me back in 1999 to carry on running the Fort. "It is in your blood... and is your destiny!" he said.

I'd also like to dedicate this book to my father, Sam'l Paul Arnold, who was crazy enough in the first place to build a fort as our home, and to adopt a little bear in 1963 who made her home at The Fort with us.

....

This book would not have been possible without my creative team, Lester Goodman, Creative Director, Barbara Scott-Goodman, Designer, Mary Goodbody, Editor, and Christina Wald, Illustrator. Thank you for capturing my love of Sissy and her adventures at The Fort!

Preface

When I was a little girl and living with my dad, mom and brother, Keith, in an apartment above my parents' restaurant in Colorado, a bear cub came to live with us. Her name was Sissy Bear and she and I became such good friends that I sometimes cuddled up against her warm, furry shoulder for a nap.

This is the story of how Sissy came to live at The Fort and how she affected our lives. It's also the story of the early days of The Fort, a restaurant that's inside of a real adobe fort!

Today, we serve what we call "new foods of the Old West" at the restaurant. We also teach school kids about the history of Colorado's forts through a school tour program, and sponsor many family events organized by a non-profit foundation called Tesoro Cultural Center.

My dad and mom opened The Fort in the foothills southwest of Denver, Colorado, in 1963, and I run it these days. It's always been a magical place and Keith and I spent a wonderful childhood there. Not only were there mountains to climb and endless open spaces for us to run and play in, we had dogs and cats — and a friendly bear!

How Did a *Real* Bear Come to Live at The Fort?

Sissy Bear was just a two months old when she came to live with my family at The Fort near Morrison, Colorado. It was 1963 and the Canadian black bear cub, who had been through a lot in her short life, was in urgent need of a home. No one knows what happened to her mother, but we do know that before she ended up at the Denver Zoo, Sissy was the property of a down-on-its-luck roadside game farm. During the short weeks with the game farm, Sissy was declawed, not given enough to eat, and hit repeatedly with a pipe whenever she gnawed on something to relieve the pain of growing teeth — like a puppy does. Before the game farm closed its doors for good, Sissy caught her first break in life. She was given to the zoo.

Malnourished and abused, the cub was named "Sissy" by the zoo's staff and carefully nursed back to health. The zoo's bear experts knew she could not survive among the other bears because a clawless bear cannot defend herself and so they reached out to a well known animal trainer named Tuffy Trusdale, who had a wrestling bear named Victor and knew a lot about how to handle bears.

Tuffy was a kind man — despite his reputation as a bear and alligator wrestler — but he already had a tame bear. He told the zoo that although he could not take her, he would find a home for the abandoned cub.

In those days, Tuffy and his wife traveled through the West in an old school bus with three alligators in a specially outfitted trunk and their trained bear, who rode with the people. Victor was a handsome Canadian Black Bear who stood six feet, five inches tall and weighed in at over 700 pounds. He was jet black except for a beautiful "V" of white hair on his chest.

As they traveled, Tuffy and his wife would set up a small circus tent and demonstrate to large and small audiences how to wrestle a bear and a few alligators. Victor wore a muzzle to prevent unintended nips and bites and happily tussled with Tuffy. Once he'd wrestled with the bear, Tuffy welcomed audience members to try, too. Victor often stuck his tongue through the muzzle's mesh to lick his rivals on the face!

INDIANA PACERS vs UTAH STARS

APRIL 2, 8:05

Final Home Game Of Regular Season

With Special Half-Time Show
Featuring Victor The Wrestling Bear

(Victor is on the right)

Sissy made friends with everyone. Clockwise from top: Sissy and my dad, Sam Arnold; Sissy and my grandmother, Katherine Arnold; Sissy with Keith, my brother; The poster advertises one of Tuffy's and Victor's shows.

In the spring of 1963, Tuffy and my dad, Sam Arnold, came to an agreement that brought Tuffy's traveling show to The Fort for the summer. The restaurant had only recently opened and Dad, an advertising guy who recognized a good opportunity when he saw one, knew the bear and alligators would be a draw and help put us on the map.

The Fort is an exact replica of Colorado's old Bent's Fort and back then, before the highway was built, was a good hour's drive from Denver. Dad had moved our family to the second floor of the adobe building, away from Denver, and my brother Keith and I were excited to be living in a "real" fort. We were even more excited when Tuffy and company set up their tent in our courtyard.

For a dollar, anyone could wrestle with Victor for five minutes. I tried it when I was just nine years old. We'd returned from church and I was wearing my Sunday best, but that didn't stop me. Victor was very gentle with children, but if a teenager or grown man decided to "show him they meant business," Victor would quickly wrestle them to the ground and sit on top of them, all the while offering big, slurpy kisses through the front of his muzzle. We'd laugh till our bellies hurt, and then everyone would cheer for Victor!

For his next act, Tuffy brought out a large mat and two alligators. Wearing nothing but a tight Speedo bathing suit, this good-looking, muscular guy with a meticulously groomed goatee, announced that he would muzzle the alligators.

Keith and I would sit on the vigas — protruding beams — that extended over the courtyard and watch Tuffy wrestle his alligators. One time, we heard a few loud "snaps" and then saw blood everywhere. Oh no! Was our friend injured? Very quickly, Tuffy leapt up victorious. Both gators were muzzled, despite the fact that one had bitten its own tail, the source of the spurting blood. Tuffy tended to the wounded tail, which healed without a trace.

One day late in the summer, Tuffy and his wife had to go away for a weekend and left Keith and me in charge of feeding the rapacious reptiles and hosing them down with fresh water every day. I'll never forget opening the trunk where they lived. The first thing you'd notice was the loud hissing as the beasts opened their powerful jaws in anticipation of the raw chickens we had to feed them. We'd toss a piece of chicken into the waiting mouths, watch them snap shut for an instant before they opened again with a forceful — and frightening — hisssss!

It was scary. The alligators were six to seven feet long and as a nine-year-old I was a lot smaller than that. It occurred to me that I could easily be a tasty snack for them! Keith, who was two years older, was equally wary of my vulnerability and made sure I stood far enough back so as to be perfectly safe. Soon after that week-end, Tuffy got the call from the Denver Zoo asking him to help find a home for Sissy. His solution was to recommend that the zoo issue a zoo license to The Fort and he would teach our family how to train and handle a wild animal. Sissy would live in the courtyard at The Fort. A little girl's dream come true!

Sissy Bear's Home at The Fort

We were about to get a bear! But, we wondered, where does a bear sleep? Bears feel secure in caves so my father had a cave blasted out of the red rock next to the open courtyard at The Fort. For privacy, we built a wooden structure called a lean-to in front of the cave's entrance. We filled the cave with clean hay and straw and thought we were done. But wait! Bears like water so we made her a swimming pool, which actually was a metal horse trough, complete with a colorful beach ball floating on the surface. Dad had a chain link fence installed to separate Sissy from the guests who walked through the courtyard on their way to the restaurant. Finally, we hung a sign on the fence that said "Please don't feed your fingers to the bear, as her diet is carefully planned."

Before Sissy arrived, my dad had befriended and then hired a Lakota Indian chief named Chief Big Cloud. We had met the chief, who was also known as Charlie Wrangle, at Mt. Rushmore and he and his wife, Bell, came to live at The Fort. They talked with our guests about the Lakota, Native Americans, and The Fort's adobe building. From her first day, Sissy and Charlie shared a strong bond that never wavered. He adored her, and the feeling was mutual.

Chief Big Cloud, a Lakota Indian chief, formed a life-long bond with Sissy.

What to Feed a Bear?

To establish trust and a true attachment during training, Tuffy told us not to give Sissy any food until she took it from our hand. We gave her water, but no food and after three days, she finally took a small piece from my hand. Victory! She never hesitated to eat anything from that day forward. And she was never deprived, either!

Bears are primarily vegetarians, so we gave Sissy a tub filled with lettuce, apples, cauliflower, beans...just about anything that the restaurant's chefs were prepping for dinner. Sissy got the trimmings as well as bigger chunks. We added cod liver oil and several raw eggs to prevent dry skin and keep her coat shining, and then we'd fill the rest of the tub with dog food. She was a very happy bear!

She was even happier when we put a buffalo bone in the tub, which she loved to chew. And we discovered she had a real sweet tooth. Her favorites? Bright red maraschino cherries!

That fall our neighbor Mrs. Enabow taught me to make a hearty porridge with a recipe from her native Sweden. It was a thick mixture of flour, milk, butter, and cinnamon that resembled oatmeal. Once cooked, I added even more butter and sugar and decided it probably resembled the porridge Goldilocks sampled in the fairy tale.

I had porridge and I had a bear! When I offered her some porridge, Sissy eagerly slurped it up with her surprisingly long tongue. When she pulled the sweet, gluey concoction back into her mouth, it stuck to the roof of her mouth and she'd use her tongue, wiggle her jaw, and make funny, contorted faces as she worked to guide the porridge down her throat. I'd roll on the ground, laughing so hard it hurt.

Sissy and I became close in those early years. I'd rush off the school bus, race to the courtyard and flop down to take a nap with my warm, furry friend. After our nap, we'd wrestle. Sissy knew I was a defenseless kid and was gentle during this rough housing. She occasionally nipped my arm, but never hard enough to break the skin.

Kissed by a Bear

Tuffy taught us to stand straight and tall with a maraschino cherry held loosely between our lips. We then encouraged Sissy to stand on her rear legs, put her forepaws on our shoulders and gently take the cherry from our mouth. And now we'd been kissed by a bear! Sissy loved this trick, primarily because she was so crazy about maraschino cherries. Of course, Tuffy warned, don't accidently swallow the cherry or let it drop from your mouth. Sissy would be expecting it.

We opened The Fort to school children learning about the history of their state. Bent's Fort had been an international fur trade fort that operated in the Colorado territory in the early 1800s. For Colorado kids, it's significant and teachers were only too happy to organize field trips to the building that was a faithful replica of the old building. At age 10, I was allowed to lead some of these school tours, dressed in period dress — I even showed my fellow classmates around Bent's Fort. At the end of the tour, the kids lined up and we gave each a maraschino cherry. Enter Sissy, who worked her way down the line of excited kids, gently taking the cherry from each one. Needless to say, the kids loved being "kissed" by a bear and in return they loved Sissy. Later, we discovered that a tamed bear had lived in the courtyard of the original Bent's Fort.

Sissy also loved orange soda. We left the cap on the bottle of soda and then poked tiny holes in it with a small hammer and nail. We taught Sissy to stand on her hind

My dad holds a bottle of orange soda for Sissy to drink. Sissy "kisses" my grandmother, Katherine Arnold, who is completely charmed!

legs and hold the soda bottle between her front paws — all the while standing at the restaurant's bar. It would take some work and time for her to suck the miniscule amounts of soda through the holes and she'd be quite content to stand there for long periods, worrying the soda into her mouth. There still is a 1964 photo of Sissy hanging in The Fort to this day. She's standing at the bar, holding the soda bottle to her mouth. The picture has led some to believe she was drinking beer. It would never occur to us to give our bear alcohol, nor is it a good idea to *ever* let a wild animal drink beer or any other alcohol. At least not if you value your life.

Sissy loved orange soda and other treats. Clockwise from the top, my dad and a Fort guest "kissing" Sissy; Keith taking Sissy for a walk; Sissy happily stands at The Fort's bar, nursing a bottle of orange soda!

When business was slow, Keith and I led Sissy up The Fort's driveway to the road, keeping her happy with a constant stream of sweet cherries. The sight of a bear and a couple of kids on the side of the road convinced a number of drivers to stop, and we would talk up The Fort. Our goal was to lead them, Pied Piper-like, down the drive, through the courtyard and into the restaurant for a meal.

Sissy wore a thick chain around her neck, which we used like a leash on a dog. Every now and then, she'd break the chain and we'd find her on top of the huge red rock above her cave. No problem. We'd let her roam free for a few hours; she never strayed too far. The Fort was her home.

Sissy climbs into my dad's favorite car!

The Wild in the Bear

Tuffy taught us that bears are always wild and so it's important to never ignite their wild instincts. For instance, don't play tag or encourage them to run or chase you. You cannot outrun a bear; they are solid muscle and very fast and so if they see you running away from them, they will run after you — and catch you. As children growing up in bear country, we were taught to confront a bear head on and never turn our back to them or run, should we come upon one in the woods or on hiking trail. If a bear charges, we were told, huff back and stand your ground.

Bears have extremely sensitive noses and can smell food on your clothing, we learned. As tame as she was, Sissy could get angry if she thought we were hiding food from her, Tuffy said. This is why we held our hands high over our heads when we approached her, showing her we had no food. We'd let her sniff us all over and even stick her nose in our jeans' pockets. If we had food in a pocket, it went directly to Sissy.

Do Bears Hibernate?

Sissy never hibernated. In fact, bears don't sleep all winter, even in the wild. They slow down, sleep through the worse of the cold weather and wake up several times. They don't eat much but live off the body fat they accumulate over the summer and fall.

Sissy was well fed all year long and yet she slowed down a lot in the winter. She slept more than usual and was sluggish. When spring arrived, she enthusiastically rejoined life in The Fort's courtyard, looking matted and itchy. We brushed her out, much as you'd groom a dog, taking great care with her undercoat, which needed the most help.

Sissy and Lobo: A Love Story

When we were kids, we housed a menagerie at The Fort: three or four German shepherds, an oversized tom cat named Big John, pet rabbits — even a "de-scented" skunk named Flower, who was my mother's special pet. She had grown up on a farm in Georgia and loved all animals, a passion she passed on to her kids. I even once nursed an injured young coyote back to health

Other than Sissy, by far our most beloved pet was Lobo, a large and gentle German shepherd that we'd rescued from a bad situation. We were driving through Denver as a family one day when we saw a couple of teenagers dragging a howling German shepherd down the street, his haunches bound with phone wire that was cutting into his flesh and causing him to cry out in pain. My dad pulled over and

offered the kids twenty bucks for the dog, a lofty sum in the early 1960s. Keith and I made room for him in the backseat and from that first car ride, Lobo, as we called him, was devoted to us. We got him home (we had not yet moved to The Fort), fed him and called the vet. Luckily he wasn't badly hurt.

When we moved to The Fort, Lobo was in dog heaven! He roamed the acres sur-rounding the building and acted as faithful watchdog when the sun went down. He was a loving companion for Keith and me and Keith taught him how to ride on the back of his dirt bike. He reminded me of the noble Rin Tin Tin, the canine hero of one of my favorite television shows.

When Sissy arrived to join our menagerie, she immediately fell in love with Lobo and he with her. Perhaps they sensed that both shared a history of abuse or maybe they just liked to play together. And play they did! Both were young and full of energy and they'd wrestle in the courtyard, alarming some of our restaurant guests who thought Sissy would kill the dog. At the crucial moment, Lobo would leap free of Sissy's grasp, jump on her back and nip the bear on the back, his teeth bared. Our guests would applaud. And then Sissy and Lobo would lie down next to each other to take a little nap! Or the bear might amble over to a nearby picnic table and sit on the bench, like a human. (She also sometimes climbed the stairs to our living room and sat on the sofa, short bear legs dangling over the edge.)

Lobo lived with us for a few more years until one morning when he didn't return from his nightly rounds. We found him in a nearby field, severely injured. We rushed him to the vet, who surmised he'd been attacked by a group of coyotes or maybe raccoons. The vet tended to his multiple wounds, which were infected, but to no avail. Lobo died later that night.

In the middle of the night, Sissy woke us howling and whining. We warmed up some milk and honey for her, hoping it would calm her down. When the vet called in the morning with the sad news, we realized Lobo had died just about the time Sissy was so distraught. She knew!

Sissy grieved for her friend for months, refusing to eat much and moping around. As the years went by, she tried playing with the other dogs, but they weren't Lobo. Occasionally, wild bears came in search of Sissy, primarily young males looking for a mate. They didn't interest Sissy. We weren't always pleased with these suitors. One nearly made it into our smoke oven when we were smoking turkeys for our Thanksgiving guests!

In the end, Lobo was Sissy's true love. The two really had cared for each other — happily they now are together in heaven.

How Long Did Sissy Live at The Fort?

Sissy Bear lived a good, long life for a bear. She came to live at The Fort in 1963 and died in 1982 at age 19. She made her home in The Fort's courtyard for those years, charming guests, sleeping in the mountain sunshine, and eating well.

By the late 1960s, I moved back East and didn't visit The Fort very often. My father and brother stayed in Denver and although another family had come to live at and run The Fort, Dad and Keith visited our beloved bear every few months. The visits were long and rewarding; the three of them stayed close until Sissy died.

When I visited Sissy after a number of years living on the East Coast, I confess to feeling a little afraid. She had grown up to be a strapping black bear, weighing about 700 pounds. She was still gentle and happy in her domesticated home at The Fort; the family that had taken over The Fort had kids who had done a good job taking care of the bear. Sissy sensed my apprehension, just as horses know when someone is a little leery, and I held back. My days of napping with the bear were behind me!

I was on the East Coast going to school when I got the news that Sissy had died peacefully of heart failure. It broke my heart to hear about her death. To this day I believe her heart had broken when Lobo died and, even so many years later, she herself died of a broken heart.

Sissy's Legacy at The Fort

I'm happy to say that today I run The Fort. Every day I am surrounded by wonderful and happy memories as well as a growing, vibrant and exciting community. Guests tell me their own Sissy stories, often recalling when they were "kissed by the bear" or helped feed her. I love hearing about Sissy and surely both her and Lobo's spirits live on at The Fort.

Guests have asked me for more information about Sissy. One woman asked me to put the information on our website so she could show her grandchildren that a bear really did live at The Fort. And so I wrote this little book to share my memories of Sissy.

We sell Sissy Bear toys at The Fort. I hope if you buy one, you'll take good care of your own Sissy and remember the real one when you play with her and snuggle with her when you're sleepy. Come back and visit us, bring your little bear, and tell me your stories about your adventures with Sissy!